Letters to My Corruption © 2023 Victoria Clark

Presentation by *BookLeaf Publishing*

Web: www.bookleafpub.com

E-mail: info@bookleafpub.com

ISBN: 9789358318319

First edition 2023

Letters to My Corruption

Victoria Clark

BookLeaf Publishing

India | USA | UK

DEDICATION

I dedicate this book to my Grandma Judy. Grandma, you have always been my rock in everything I do. I appreciate all your help all these years and for that I thank you!

ACKNOWLEDGEMENT

Thank you to the people who entered my life to teach me valuable lessons about growth. Without you, none of this would be possible. Thank you to the family and friends who stuck by my side and were always great supporters throughout all of my past lessons. Last but not least, thank you to me. Victoria, you have grown so much! I am very proud of the person you are becoming, even when you feel like who you are now is not enough.

PREFACE

Your words cut me like a knife as I simply just walked past you. Instead of backing away I decided to keep walking back and forth, stumbling and running into the knife until I felt numb. This book was brought on by my ability to finally grow and let go of the past trauma I have/still currently deal with. This book is meant for you to see the unhealed me, the learning me and the healed me. I hope these poems can help you move forward, move on or start to heal like it has helped me.

Old Pain

All these years,
I couldn't help but cry.
You!
My own father!
How I wished it would end.

The pain.
The hurt.
The never-ending abuse that you would send.
You hurt me.
You hurt us.
Oh will this ever cease to end.

I hate you,
I truly do.
How could you do this to our family?
How could you make my mother feel so blue?

I left.
I ran.
Never speaking to you again.
You!
My own father!
Abusing us until the very end.

Realizing You

It took me years to realize your pain.
Your parents didn't care for you that much,
In that instance I felt the same.

You took your anger out on us,
An anger that left a bruise.
The anger of your childhood,
You desperately wanted to lose.

I've realized now,
It's not all your fault.
I've realized now,
This was something that was taught.

Dear Dad

It was time to forgive you.
It was time to move on.
It was time to let go.
Your trauma won't affect me anymore.

I forgive you for the abuse.
I forgive you for the hatred.
I forgive you for the lost moments.
Your pain is now outdated.

Maybe.
One day.
We will be able to talk.
Father and daughter.
Oh that would be a shock.
That's something for wishful thinkers,
Good thing I am logical.

All I know now is that I am going to be ok.
That is something I always hoped for.
Maybe one day.

Ignored Pain

You were my safety net.
Something to protect me from the pain.
Even when things were bad, I could run to you.
Things were bad all the time though.

As years passed by,
I realized you weren't my safety net.
You were safe compared to what we dealt with.
Instead,
you condoned the abuse we faced each and
every day.

You ignored the pain.
You ignored the ridicule.
You ignored us.
The anger I held towards that is the resentment I
have today.
Yes, you kept us "safe".
You also let us stay in pain.
You watched as we tried to survive and instead
of helping us, you left everything the same.

Silent Resentment

How could you do this to me?
You molded me into the person I said I didn't
want to be.
Overly caring.
Overly helpful.
Always getting hurt in the long run.

How could you do this to me?
I watched as you bent over backwards for a
cowardly man.
A man who beat and hurt you again and again.
You always smiled though,
Always happy.

Why didn't you stop?
Now I can't stop either.
I'm on a loop of codependency that I wish I
could drop.

Dear Mom

You were just a child.
Sixteen?
Pregnant with me?
You didn't know how to parent.
You didn't know how to leave abuse.

All that being said,
I forgive you.
Scared for your life.
Scared of change
Scared of new things.
In that aspect,
You and I are the same.

Wishing things were different won't change a
thing.
So instead of dwelling in the past,
I forgive you for the whole thing.
I forgive you for your absence.
I forgive you for your tolerance.
I forgive you for it all.

Unexpected Pain

You were something unexpected.

It was kind of like when you get a good grade on
a test you didn't study for.
It was kind of like when you turn on the radio
and it's playing your favorite song.
It was kind of like when everything in your life
is going to shit and that one person pops up
unexpectedly.

That was you.

You were unexpected happiness.
You were unexpected joy.
So why was I surprised when you unexpectedly
hurt me?
You unexpectedly gave up.
You unexpectedly threw away our friendship.
You unexpectedly didn't show up.

You have always been unexpected so why was I
so confused?
You have always been unexpected news.

Hidden memories

I erased you from my memory.
I erased you from my soul.
Why can't I forget you?
That is something I will never know.

Bits and pieces of memories...
They are always floating near.
I try and try to forget them,
but for some reason I hold them dear.

Hidden, you are.
Hiding in my mind.
I want to forget you but,
I don't really have the time.

I hide you as I walk.
I hide you as I talk.
Your memories hurt me,
I just wish I could forget.

The happy ones.
The sad ones.
All of it is a mess.

You broke my heart in two.

You probably don't even care.
You were supposed to be my friend,
But instead, you are totally unaware.

I long for you to come back.
All of this feels wrong.
A part of me is missing,
This all just sounds like a depressing song.

No longer my best friend.
No longer my sister.
The tears I cry today,
will be the tears I cry forever.

Dear Ex-Bestfriend

My life was at a standstill.
I wondered if I would ever move.
The memory of you haunted me,
your memory is all I wanted to lose.

It took me a while to realize,
It's okay to lose hope.
Some friendships don't last,
Some friendships are meant to outgrow.

I think of our memories now with a smile on my
face.
These memories we have,
No one can replace.

I forgive you for leaving.
I forgive you for covering up your tattoo.
You did what you felt was right,
You did what you had to do.

I love you so much, I always will.
That's something that will never change, that's
something I will always feel
You were my best friend,
The best I ever had,

Nothing will ever be the same.
I wish you the best, in everything you do.
It's time to let go now,
It's time to see this through.

Lover's Pain

Broken.
Scared.
Wondering what's next.

To lose you.
My love.
My favorite.
My life.
My everything.

I still sit at that table where it all ended.
I envision how the conversation would have
gone if I fought for you when I didn't.
Would you have kept trying?
Or were you already done?

I thought we would be forever.
I thought you were the one.
I thought...
I thought very wrong.

Webs of Torture

We were toxic.
Our poisonous webs trapped us as we kept
trying to move.
Frozen into the moment.
We looked at each other in pain but kept on
fighting.

I thought I was the strong one but that wasn't
true.
You were the one to leave,
That takes much more strength.
Staying is easy.
Staying is the easier way.

We both didn't want to stay though.
We wanted it to end.
We wanted excitement.
We wanted love.
We didn't want to pretend.

It was love at first though.
Somewhere along the way,
The love turned into hate.
I wish there was some way you could've stayed.

Dear Ex-Girlfriend

You were by far the best person I met.
Or at least someone hard to forget.
Letting go was hard.
It took me years to finally let you go.

I finally let go of who we were and who we were
meant to be.
It wasn't easy,
That is something everyone could see.

The sad part is,
Part of me will always love you.
Or maybe part of me will always love who you
used to be.
Or who we used to be.

The end of the road is near,
I'm afraid to say.
It's finally time to figure out who I am, such a
crushing gasp of fresh air that was today.

Rival Pain

15

Growing up with you was a battle.
Not because you were difficult, but because our
father pinned us against one another.
Who was better?
Who was stronger?
Who was faster?
Everyday was a contest.

As we got older,
Things like that never stopped.
One day though, I decided to sink like a rock
I realized that I was done trying to compete.
How could I compete when I wasn't even whole.

You were always the whole one, even when you
didn't think so.
I was just a good pretender.
I was never better, you were.

Years of Hatred

How we are now brings me to tears.
We barely talk.
We barely text.
We are barely even near.

The way you speak to me, as if I'm not worthy,
sickens me.
I know my worth,
do you know yours?

As you kicked me while I was down, I realized it
was what we were taught.
Stick our noses up,
Always be better than the rest,
Never take no for an answer.
Never be distraught.

When does the hate stop?

Dear Brother

I know now how you felt.
Worthlessness.
Not good enough.
2nd place.

You might have felt that from others but,
I felt that from myself.
The anger.
The sadness.
It was hard to overcome.
Sometimes, it's still hard.

I never meant to make you feel that way.
I'm sorry my actions caused you to feel unheard.
I'm sorry my actions caused you to feel absurd.
You are enough.
You have always been.
I hope you know that now.
I hope you never forget it until the end.

Hurtful Pain

We never got along.
We just never got each other.
Always so different.
Always looking at a different picture.

As we grew up,
we tried to get along.
Your words and actions would burn small holes
in my soul.
The burns wouldn't stop,
Then suddenly my heart wasn't there anymore.

I tried for many years to understand this pain.
I tried for many years to be near.
The pain I felt from this,
makes me feel so numb.
I learned to accept "it is what it is" when us
being sisters should have been enough.

Madness

Your hurtful words.
My actions never enough.
I try to help.
I try to be tough.

Your anger controls you.
It consumes you whole.
Anger has never been my friend,
It has never been in my soul.

Your anger turns against you in every step you
make.
Your anger comes at me like something I cannot
take.
I never want to be like you, I hate to even say.
Always angry,
Always enraged.

Dear Sister

We may never see eye to eye,
That is ok.
We may never come to our senses,
We will never be the same.

No one is perfect,
That I know for sure.
Regardless of what happens,
I love you with my whole heart.

My sister.
My opposite.
Things will never be clear.

We may never see eye to eye but,
I will always want you near.

Self Pain

The anger I have for you.
Why do you choose to live like this?
Always giving,
Giving until there is no end.

It's a cycle,
Something you seem to never break.
Loss,
Heartbreak,
Giving your all to people who seem to not care
if you are awake.

Oh, Victoria...
When will you ever learn?
You aren't supposed to live for them.
This world, is yours.

The pain you feel doesn't come from the people
you come across.
The pain you feel comes from you and all the
pain you allowed them to cause.

Your pain.
My pain.
Our pain.

Why do we do this to ourselves?
Oh, Victoria...
When will we ever finally get over this trauma
and move on to get some help?

The Past

Growing up as you,
It was hard as it could be.
You never lived for yourself.
You never wanted to be set free.

Family.
Friends.
A cycle on repeat.

You were weak in a world that wanted you to
speak.
Speak up Victoria,
I know you can do it.
Speak up Victoria,
Why do you put yourself through it?

Dear Me

You stood up for yourself.
You decided to be better.
You finally gave up your pain,
You finally decided to write that letter.

You let go of others and their opinions of you.
You let go of toxicness and try to never let it get
to you.
You try for you, and that's all that matters.

There is still some sadness,
That's pretty normal though.
Once you finally let go of the past,
You will be able to fully grow.

You got this Victoria!
I believe in you!
I know your worth,
I know you will see it through.